Animal Habitats

The Mouse in the Barn

Text by Robert Burton

Photographs by
Oxford Scientific Films

Gareth Stevens Publishing
Milwaukee

Contents

Note: The use of a capital letter for a mouse's name means that it is a *species* of mouse (for example, House Mouse). The use of a lower case, or small, letter means that it is a member of a larger *group* of mice.

A House Mouse meets a cow. A cow shed is a good place to live because the mouse can steal the cows' food.

A sack of grain provides plenty of food.

Mice around the world

Many kinds of animals live in barns and other buildings, where they find food and shelter. They include House Sparrows, pigeons, flies, cockroaches, and several *species* of mice and rats. Most of these animals are called *commensals*, because they share our food and live with us. Some carry disease. This also means that they are *pests*. They are not popular, and we try to keep them out of buildings.

There are about three hundred species of mice living in all parts of the world except the polar regions. One species in particular is an important commensal because it regularly lives in barns, where it destroys stored food. This is the House Mouse.

House Mice originally lived in the *steppes* of Asia and around the Mediterranean Sea. As soon as the people living in this part of the world started to grow grain during the New Stone Age, about ten thousand years ago, the mice took advantage of this new supply of food. They ate the crops in the fields and came into houses and barns to eat stored grain. Then, as farming spread across Europe and Asia, the House Mouse followed. House Mice came to Britain with settlers from the continent of Europe before the time of the Romans, over two thousand years ago.

From their original home in the steppes, House Mice have spread to all sorts of places. They live on the edges of hot deserts, in sugarcane plantations, on mountains, and along the edge of the frozen Antarctic. However, they are not often found in dense forests.

When Europeans explored other parts of the world they carried House Mice with them. Mice were *introduced* to North America and Australia by the first colonists, who carried the mice accidentally in cargoes of grain and other food. Similarly, House Mice have been taken in ships to many islands around the world. An American ship took House Mice to Fiji in 1840, and seal hunters introduced them to the Antarctic island of South Georgia 150 years ago. However, they reached the Galapagos Islands in the Pacific only a few years ago.

The Wood Mouse is also called the Long-tailed Field Mouse. It comes indoors in winter.

The Deer Mouse sometimes lives in barns and other buildings.

The House Mouse is not the only mouse to eat crops in the fields and to come into barns and houses to eat stored food. In Europe the Wood Mouse, also called the Long-tailed Field Mouse, becomes a commensal only in winter. So does its close relative, the Yellow-necked Mouse. Here in North America, the Deer Mouse, which looks and behaves much like a Wood Mouse, also comes indoors to steal food. Africa is the home of several commensal mice, including the Multi-mammate Mouse, the Spiny Mouse, and the Grass Mouse.

The Spiny Mouse of Africa has stiff, prickly fur.
It often steals grain and other food.

Footprints and other signs show that this beam is used regularly for crossing the barn.

Living with people

Although many House Mice live outside, some move into buildings and spend the rest of their lives indoors. Generations then pass without a single mouse venturing into the open air. Other species, like the Wood Mouse, are mainly outdoor mice. But a few come indoors for food when their natural food becomes scarce in winter.

The barn is a perfect home for a mouse. Here a farmer stores grain or food for the farm animals in bins and sacks, so a mouse in a barn is surrounded by food. It finds all it needs without having to walk far. This means that barns can become *infested* with many large mice.

Mice are good climbers, so they can scamper up the crossbeams that take them to their regular overhead routes across the barn.

House Mice can also be found in some strange places, such as refrigerated rooms and coal mines where they live on crusts and crumbs left by the miners. Mice in cold rooms live in total darkness and temperatures of 15 degrees Fahrenheit (-10 degrees Centigrade). They feed on frozen meat and grow thick fur to keep warm.

Signs to look for

If you go into a barn or a shed where seeds and plants are kept, or anywhere else that you think mice may be living, you can easily tell that they are there. You will certainly find signs of their activities. Trails of footprints, and marks where their tails have dragged in the dust, show where the mice have their regular paths. Dirty black smears show where they have squeezed along walls and under beans. Here and there, the mice leave small piles of black droppings and crumbs of half-eaten food. There will also be a stale, "mousey" smell if there are lots of mice around.

Once you have found some signs, wait quietly and patiently. You may hear squeaking and rustling or chewing noises. This shows that the mice are active, and you may soon see one come out.

Droppings are the most obvious signs that mice are around.

The Wood Mouse has a very long tail and is white underneath.

The mouse's body

Mice are actually attractive little animals! They have shiny black eyes, round ears, and long tails. They belong to a group of *mammals* called rodents. Rats, squirrels, chipmunks, and beavers are also rodents. They have long front teeth, called *incisors*, which are used for gnawing. Incisors have sharp, chisel edges for gnawing hard things like nutshells and wood. Unlike other teeth, incisors grow continuously, so they stay sharp and long even though gnawing hard things wears them away. The cheek teeth in the back of the mouth are blunt and are used for chewing food.

Mice have sharp front teeth for gnawing and blunt back teeth for chewing. The gap between is called the diastema.

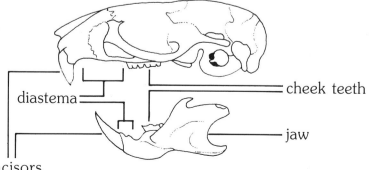

Between the incisors and the cheek teeth there is a gap called the *diastema*. The rodent pulls the skin of its cheek into the diastema and closes off its mouth. Then it can gnaw on nutshells, and other hard things, without swallowing the pieces. This is how a House Mouse makes holes in walls and doors so that it can get into cupboards.

It is not easy to tell which species a mouse belongs to when it scurries across the floor. If, however, you can hold one in your hand, there are several things to look for. (You can safely pick up a House Mouse by its tail, but this is cruel to a Wood Mouse or Yellow-necked Mouse because the skin of their tails comes off easily.)

House Mice have grayish-brown fur which may be paler on the underside of the body. An adult House Mouse weighs just over half an ounce (18 grams) and measures 2 1/2 to 3 1/2 inches (70 to 90 mm) from the tip of its nose to the base of the tail. The tail is slightly shorter than the rest of the animal. House Mice living in warm places have longer tails. The extra bare skin on a long tail acts as a radiator, giving out heat and helping keep the mouse cool.

The Wood Mouse and Yellow-necked Mouse are somewhat larger than the House Mouse. They weigh from 0.6 to 1 ounce (18 to 30 grams) and measure 3 to 5 inches (80 to 130 mm). They also look prettier because their ears and eyes are larger and their coats are an attractive brown with yellow on the *flanks*. (The dull grayish-brown fur of the House Mouse looks dirty by comparison.) The underside of the body is white, with a yellow patch between the front legs. The patch is small or even absent in the Wood Mouse, but it is much larger and forms a broad collar in the Yellow-necked Mouse. This is how it gets its name.

A curious mouse gets a better view by sitting up on its hind legs.

A mouse gets an extra grip by wrapping its tail around the cord as it descends.

Movement

Mice have five toes on each of their front and back feet. You can see the toes clearly if you look for footprints in mud or thick dust. The marks of the claws may be visible, too. Mice walk or run when they are not in a hurry. A good sense of balance and sharp claws help mice to climb up walls. They can also run along thin wires. Their feet give them a good grip, and the tail swings from side to side for balance, the way that we wave our arms for balance when walking on a line.

The hind feet get a firm grip as the mouse climbs.

A Yellow-necked Mouse makes a spectacular leap.

If mice are frightened, they race for safety in zig-zags and cover the ground in 18-inch (45-cm) leaps until they disappear from sight. Wood Mice and Yellow-necked Mice can jump up to 36 inches (90 cm) vertically into the air. Zig-zags and jumps make it difficult for *predators* to catch mice. If you move some boxes where mice are hiding, they leap in all directions like tiny kangaroos.

Bulging eyes help the mouse see danger approaching from any direction, but its eyesight is not very good except for detecting movements.

Senses

A mouse has large eyes and ears, a sensitive nose, and a set of long whiskers. These are four sense organs for helping the mouse find its way around, search for food, and detect danger.

The mouse's large round ears are constantly moving to pick up tiny sounds that may mean danger.

Although their eyes are large and bright, eyesight is not an important sense for mice. They are short-sighted and you can creep up on a mouse without its noticing until you make a sudden movement. Their hearing is excellent, however, and the slightest noise will make the mouse disappear in a flash. Whenever a mouse is awake, its ears are constantly moving to pick up the slightest sound from any direction. It can hear *ultrasonic* sounds, which are too high-pitched for us to hear.

Every now and then, a mouse lifts its nose and sniffs the air for danger. The sense of smell is also important for finding and testing food, and for communicating with other mice.

It's whiskers tell a mouse if there are any obstacles in front of it. The mouse spreads out its whiskers in front of its nose as it walks, in the same way as we hold out our arms in the dark. The whiskers will also tell the mouse if a hole is wide enough to get through.

As this mouse approaches a gap in the wall, its whiskers spread out like a fan to warn it when it is going to bump its nose.

Mice are wasteful eaters and leave plenty of crumbs.

Food and feeding

Mice are basically plant eaters. They also often catch insects and other tiny animals. The House Mouse eats mainly seeds, which is why it is so much at home in barns where grain is stored. One mouse eats about 100 grains of wheat each day. House Mice that live in the countryside eat the seeds of grass and other low-growing plants. When they eat fruit, they leave the soft flesh and only nibble the seeds.

A mouse sits up on its back legs and holds its food in its front paws while nibbling it. It chews each grain carefully and pauses every now and then to look around for danger. When it is eating grain, it spills tiny fragments.

When people first began to grow grains, House Mice found that they were a better source of food than wild plants, so they moved into the fields. After harvesting, the crops were bundled into bales before being thrashed and the grain stored in barns. Then the mice moved into the bales and barns. The stored grain was the farmers' food for the winter. The mice also found the grain useful because their natural food in the countryside is hard to find in winter.

House Mice have learned to eat all kinds of things since they started to live in buildings. They will steal any food that is left uncovered in the kitchen and dig up bulbs growing on the window sill. Mice also eat some surprising things. They nibble soap in the bathroom and chew wallpaper to get the glue that makes it stick to the wall. They will even gnaw the plaster off the wall.

Mice often eat soap because it is rich in fats.

Berries are a favorite for mice living in the countryside.

Although mice like to drink if there is water around, they can survive for a long time without water. They can live on stored flour without drinking because there is enough moisture in the flour for their needs.

Wood Mice and Yellow-necked Mice eat the same sorts of things as House Mice. When they are living in fields and woods, their main food is seeds. They also eat caterpillars and buds when seeds become scarce in spring. Wood Mice and Yellow-necked Mice especially like nuts. Nuts take a long time to eat because the mouse has to gnaw a hole in the shell and reach the kernel inside. You can sometimes find empty nutshells which mice have left. Squirrels split shells in half, but mice leave a neat hole with tiny toothmarks on the rim.

Mice have plenty of food in autumn, when seeds, nuts, and fruit are ripe. There is more than enough to eat, and Wood Mice, Yellow-necked Mice, and Deer Mice store some for use in the winter, when food is hard to find. The stored supplies of food are called *hoards*. House Mice do not usually make hoards unless they are living outdoors, so a hoard found indoors is probably the work of other kinds of mice.

Some mouse hoards are very large and may contain over 100 nuts or seeds. They must take a long time to gather, especially when Yellow-necked Mice make hoards among the rafters in the roof of a house. They carry the nuts, one at a time, in their mouths so that their feet are free for climbing. They can even carry horse chestnuts that weigh as much as the mice themselves.

A Wood Mouse has filled these old shoes with beans. It will come back to eat them later.

When a mouse explores a new place, it is very nervous and is alert for the first sign of danger.

Gradually, it creeps forward: looking, listening, and smelling to make sure that it is safe.

Setting up home

If a mouse decides to come into a barn for the winter, it has to explore its new home very carefully. There may be all sorts of dangers. It comes in a little way, creeping cautiously with all senses alert, and rushes out again. Then it returns, coming in a bit further, and rushes out again. Gradually the mouse gets bolder and begins to explore thoroughly. It looks into every nook and corner, smelling carefully, until it has learned the layout of its new home perfectly. It now has a network of paths that it always follows. The paths follow walls and go under sacks and boxes, so the mouse keeps out of sight as much as possible. When it has completely settled in, the mouse can find its way without thinking. If disturbed, it races blindly along a path to safety, and if an obstacle is put in the way, the mouse will run into it!

A nest keeps the mouse warm and comfortable when it is resting. This is where the babies will be born.

A mouse needs only a small *home range*, perhaps no more than 6 sq yards (5 sq m), if there is plenty of food in the barn. But if the barn is empty and there are only scraps to eat, the mouse will need a larger home range in which to find food. It will stay here for the rest of its life until the food runs out or cold weather makes it find somewhere warmer.

As soon as it is settled, the mouse makes a snug nest. It uses pieces of paper, dead leaves, old clothes, or anything else that is suitable. The mouse chews the material into shreds and piles it into an untidy heap. Inside the heap there is a hollow where the mouse sleeps, but there is no entrance. The mouse simply pushes its way in and out.

House Mice are nearly always *nocturnal*. They do not come out by day unless they are very hungry or are living in safe places where they will not be disturbed. They wake up every hour or so through the night, eat a small meal, and then go back to sleep. However, mice are more likely to be seen at dusk and dawn because they stay awake longer at these times than during the middle of the night.

Mice are usually active in the dark. They come out to feed and explore several times during the night.

A mouse has found a stranger in its territory and is driving it out.

Social life

A social order begins to form as more mice set up home in the barn. Each mouse keeps to its own home range and tries to avoid other mice. The pathways in each home range become marked with the scent of the resident mouse. Smelling its own scent makes a resident feel "at home." But a stranger smelling the resident's scent knows that it is trespassing, and it may retreat before meeting the resident. When two mice do meet, they sniff each other and, if they belong to the same family, they recognize one another's smell and pass on. If one has a different smell, it must be an intruder and the resident mouse immediately chases it out of the *territory*. The intruder usually rushes away and hides, but sometimes it is not quick enough, and the two mice fight. The intruder turns and faces its pursuer. The intruder stands on its hind feet and squeaks, which means, "I dare you to attack me." The resident may accept the challenge and attack by biting and boxing with its front paws. Or perhaps the resident may not feel like fighting, so it stops and flicks its tail. This is like shouting "Go away!" at someone a person dares not attack.

The strongest and largest males own territories that they defend against other males. Each male shares his territory with one or two females and their young. Weaker males do not have territories. They live in groups, sleeping without a real nest, and they never attack other mice. They can be recognized by their dull, scruffy fur and the wounds they have received in fights. If you catch an aggressive, territory-owning mouse, it will probably bite you. But these "outcasts" are timid and sit quietly. They are more likely to die of cold and starvation or to be eaten by predators than territory-owning mice.

Family life

Mice living in fields breed only in the summer months when the weather is warm and there is plenty of food for the family. The barn, however, holds enough food for them to breed all year. Females can start a family at the age of six weeks and they can have *litters* of four to eight babies five to ten times a year. This means that, if no babies died, a pair of mice could have over 2,500 descendants in six months!

In practice, of course, this does not happen. As the barn becomes crowded, the mouse society becomes more violent. Males in neighboring territories continually attack each other and invade each other's nests. With all this disturbance the females have fewer babies and more babies die before they grow up. Those that do survive and become adults may try to find a quieter life by leaving the barn and seeking their fortunes in the countryside.

A male mouse discovers whether the female is ready to mate by smelling her.

The male mouse mates with two or three females living in his territory. He recognizes when they are ready to mate by their smell, and he calls to them with ultrasonic squeaks to show that he is interested in mating. Before she gives birth, the female makes sure that her nest is snug and warm for her babies. She becomes aggressive when she is *pregnant* and looking after her babies after they are born. She attacks strange mice, and even the babies' father, if they come too close.

The babies are born 19 to 20 days after their mother has mated. They are pink and completely naked except for short whiskers. Their eyes and ears are closed, and they weigh only 0.03 ounce (1 gram). The mother stays in the nest to feed her babies on milk. She also keeps them warm with her own body heat, and only makes short trips away from the nest to feed.

If the babies get cold they, too, make ultrasonic squeaks and the mother adds more material to the nest to make it warmer. They also squeak if they accidentally crawl out of the nest. This alerts their mother, who will come and carry them back. Squeaking can be dangerous because it can also be heard by cats. If you see a cat staring at a wall or a pile of sacks, it is probably listening to the mice inside.

A mother mouse with her two-day-old babies. She feeds them, washes them, and keeps them warm.

When they are two weeks old, baby mice have coats of fur and are very alert. They will soon be ready to leave the nest.

The babies grow quickly. Their eyes are open and their fur coat is complete when they are two weeks old. At three weeks, the babies start to take their first steps outside the nest. Before this happens they become very active, crawling around inside the nest. Then a bold one creeps out, sniffs the air, and dashes back in. The others join it, and they explore around the nest, until they suddenly panic and all scamper back to the safety of the nest. Longer trips are taken with their mother, who walks ahead with her family following nervously. As part of their exploration, the babies start to nibble things and learn what is good to eat. When they are three weeks old, they are *weaned* from their mother's milk and eat solid food. By this time the mother is ready to start another family and the young mice have to leave and set up their own homes.

Baby mice grow very rapidly on their mother's milk until they are nearly as big as she is.

A mouse takes shelter in a milk bottle after it has been chased by a cat.

Cats and other enemies

Most mice die before they are a year old, and none live for more than one winter. Some die from disease, and others die of cold or starvation. If the weather gets too cold, several mice gather in one nest to keep each other warm. Mice in a barn will be warm and well-fed, and many live longer than outdoor mice.

Mice also have many enemies. Those living in the fields are killed and eaten by foxes, stoats, weasels, badgers, owls, and *birds of prey* such as buzzards and kestrels, which are a type of falcon. The barn is a much safer place because most of these predators never come into building. But even in a barn mice are not completely safe.

Barn Owls *roost* and nest in barns and other buildings. They catch mice they see or hear on the floor beneath them. Weasels also come into barns to catch mice. The old name for a weasel was "mouse-killer." It is so slender that it can squeeze down mouse-holes and attack mice while they are in their nests. Mice may also share the barn with their larger cousins, the rats, who sometimes eat them.

Cats, however, are the main enemies of mice. Some cats are good "mousers" and, unlike wild animals, they go on killing even when they are not hungry. Farmers keep cats to kill mice living in their barns. But mice breed too quickly for the cats to keep their numbers down.

Mice have no weapons to defend themselves against enemies. All they can do is be alert and keep under cover as much as possible. When a mouse crosses the barn floor, it uses its ears and nose to detect the first signs of danger. A mouse trapped in a corner by a cat may stand on its hind legs and squeak at it. It is not really being brave, just making a desperate last stand against a stronger enemy.

The most dangerous time for mice is when they have left their mother's nest and are looking for a home of their own. They do not have well-known pathways which they can race along to safety, and because they are still young and inexperienced, they are not quick enough to recognize the signs of danger.

Kestrels sometimes nest in barns, but they are a danger to mice living in the fields.

Two Gray Squirrels explore a roof trying to find a way in. They may find something to eat inside.

A bat clings to the ceiling. Its baby is almost hidden under its wing.

Friends and neighbors

Mice share their homes in a barn with only a few other animals. These other animals have also learned to come into buildings for food and shelter. The tiny Harvest Mouse may be brought into the barn with corn when it is harvested, but it does not stay inside for long.

Gray Squirrels sometimes come into barns and make their nests in the roof. Otherwise, bats and rats are the only mammals that regularly live in barns. You may find some bats hanging upside down in a corner of the roof, but they are more likely to be hiding out of sight. The best way to see bats is to wait outside the barn when it grows dark in the evening and watch them flying out.

Mice may have to share their food with sparrows and pigeons. These birds come into the barn to search for grain which has been spilled, and they also nest in the roof. Sparrows' nests are untidy masses of dry grass. They are nurseries for the eggs and chicks, and they are also cozy bedrooms for the winter. Pigeons make such flimsy nests that it is surprising the eggs do not fall out.

During the summer the sparrows and pigeons are joined by swallows and swifts that streak in and out of the barn at great speed. The swallow's nest is a cup of mud that is lined with hair and feathers. It is often easy to find and you can see the heads of the chicks peeping out of the nest as they wait for their parents to bring them insects to eat. The swift makes its nest of grass and feathers under the eaves or in narrow crevices where it is hard to find.

The most exciting birds found in a barn are the Barn Owl and American Kestrel. These birds of prey catch and eat small animals, so the mice have to be very careful. In some countries, farmers make special nesting places for these birds so they will help get rid of mice.

Young Barn Owls can watch mice on the floor of the barn. When they have learned to fly, they will try to catch the mice.

The Common or Brown Rat is a serious pest in many parts of the world. It often lives in the same buildings as mice.

Rats

There is no real difference between rats and mice, except that rats are much larger. Rats look and behave like mice, and they often live in barns. They may even live in the same barn, but the mice have to keep out of the rats' way or they will be killed and eaten.

Two species of rats now live in North America. Both came from central Asia, as did the House Mouse. The Black Rat probably arrived in Europe during the 11th century. This was the rat that spread the Black Death. The Brown Rat arrived much later, in about 1720. Like mice, rats traveled from Europe to North America on ships with the establishment of trade and emigration.

"Black Rat" and "Brown Rat" are inaccurate names because their color can vary. (Many Black Rats are brown and some Brown Rats are black!) The Black Rat is now often called the Ship Rat or Roof Rat and the Brown Rat is called the Common Rat. The best way of telling them apart is to look for the longer tail, the larger, pointed nose, and the hairless ears of the Ship Rat.

Ship Rats and Common Rats are now found all over the world. The Ship Rat is rarely found away from buildings, except in tropical countries. Where the two rats live together, the Common Rat lives on the floor and the Ship Rat in the roof. The Common Rat often lives in the countryside as well as in buildings. It is a serious pest on many farms, as well as in factories and houses, because of the damage it does to stored food. Being much larger than a mouse, it causes much more trouble.

Rats spread several serious diseases, such as rabies, typhus, and bubonic plaque. In the Middle Ages, bubonic plaque was called the Black Death. It was spread by the Ship Rat and killed one-third of the human population of Europe in the 14th century.

The Ship or Black Rat spread around the world before the Brown Rat.

More food is lost by spillage than is eaten by mice.

Mice as pests and pets

Many people are afraid of mice, but others do not mind seeing a mouse running around the house because they are such cute animals. They change their minds, however, when the mouse starts to nibble food or soap in the kitchen, chew carpets and sheets to make its nest, or make holes in the baseboards.

Even if the damage is not serious, people worry that the mouse's dirty habits will spread disease. House Mice can spread a kind of food poisoning called salmonella, so food ought to be kept in mouse-proof containers where mice are very common.

The problem becomes much more serious when many mice infest a barn. It is difficult to make a barn mouse-proof. Although they eat grain and other food, the main damage is caused by the mice making holes in sacks. Even when they do not eat the contents of the sack, they steal the material to make their nests. So the contents spill onto the floor and the farmer has to buy expensive new sacks. Mice also nibble apples, spoiling them so they cannot be sold.

This mouse has eaten its way through a loaf of bread.

Mice are not always easy to catch. This one is eating the bait without setting off the trap.

Even more harm can be done by a single mouse. Mice have caused fires by chewing through electric cables or gas pipes. One mouse even stopped a jumbo jet from taking off by damaging its controls.

When people want to get rid of mice, they use traps or poison. In the case of only one or two mice, a trap can get rid of them. But poisons are the only way to get rid of many mice or rats in a barn. It is important to make sure that dogs and other pets cannot get at the poison. Even if all the rats and mice are killed, new ones come in from the fields or from neighboring buildings. So there will always be a problem.

Mice make good pets because they are tame, easy to keep, and interesting to watch. There are several different color varieties, but the most common is the *albino* with pure white fur and pink eyes. Tame mice are also used by scientists to test new medicines before they are used by doctors.

White mice are cute pets which are easy to keep.

Life in the barn

Life in a barn or in any building is different from life in other *habitats* because buildings are manmade. They are not a natural habitat. And even though barns provide animals with food and shelter, many fewer kinds of animals live in barns than in other habitats. One reason is that there is usually just one kind of food (such as grain or cattle food) available in a barn, and only a few animals will be able to eat it. Another reason is that many animals (unlike mice) cannot get used to the presence of humans.

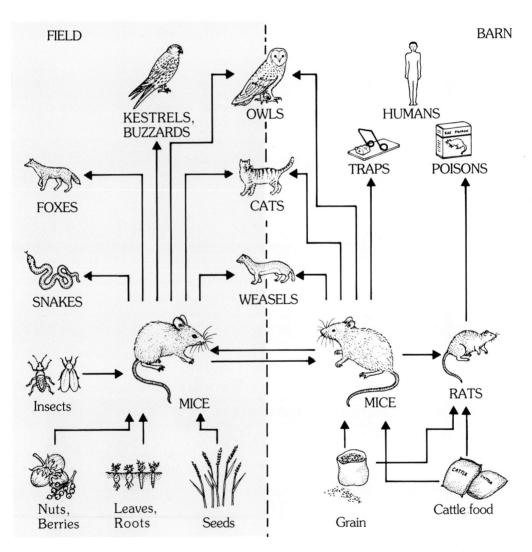

A barn and a field are very different places to live in. Mice in a barn are much safer from enemies, except humans; they have fewer kinds of food, but it is more plentiful and easier to get.

Mice find it very easy to live with people, although we may not appreciate their company.

Some animals, like squirrels, use the barn mainly for shelter, and even Wood Mice get most of their food from outside the barn. This diagram shows the difference in the lives of mice living inside and outside the barn.

Any animal that can survive in a barn will do very well. It will have food, a warm, dry shelter, few enemies, and not many other animals to compete with for the food. House Mice and rats do well in barns because they can survive on the sort of food that is stored in barns. If the food is stored in large quantities, large numbers of mice and rats can live there.

The easy life in the barn is upset when humans put out traps and poisons to kill the mice. It is difficult to get rid of all the pests in a barn because there are always more animals in the countryside or neighboring buildings waiting to move in and take over. So there will always be House Mice in barns. They are very successful animals, and they have spread around the world because they have learned to live with people.

Glossary and Index

These new words about mice appear in the text on the pages shown after each definition. Each new word first appears in the text in *italics,* just as it appears here.

Reading level analysis: SPACHE 3.7, FRY 4-5, FLESCH 82 (easy), RAYGOR 5-6, FOG 6, SMOG 3

Library of Congress Cataloging-in-Publication Data   Burton, Robert, 1941-   The mouse in the barn. (Animal habitats) Includes index.
Summary: Text and photographs depict mice feeding, breeding, and interacting with other animals in their natural habitat. 1. Mice—Juvenile literature.
[1. Mice] I. Oxford Scientific Films. II. Title. III. Series.
QL737.R666B85   1988   599.32'33   87-42614   ISBN 1-55532-330-8   ISBN 1-55532-305-7 (lib. bdg.)

North American edition first published in 1988 by Gareth Stevens, Inc., 7317 West Green Tree Road, Milwaukee, WI 53223, USA
Text copyright © 1988 by Oxford Scientific Films. All rights reserved. No part of this book may be reproduced in any form or by any means without permission in writing from Gareth Stevens, Inc.
Conceived, designed, and produced by Belitha Press Ltd., London.   Printed in the United States of America.
Series Editor: Jennifer Coldrey.   US Editor: Mark J. Sachner.   Art Director: Treld Bicknell.   Design: Naomi Games.
Line Drawings· Lorna Turpin.   Scientific Consultant: Gwynne Vevers.

The publishers wish to thank the following for permission to reproduce copyright photographs: **Oxford Scientific Films Ltd.** for front cover (Barrie E. Watts); p. 6 below and back cover (Colin Milkins); title page and pp. 2, 3, 6 above, 7, 9, 12 both, 13, 14 both, 15 above, 16 all, 17, 19, 20, 21 both, 28 below, 29 below, and 31 (John Beach/Rodger Jackman); pp. 4 and 23 (G. I. Bernard); p. 5 above (Breck P. Kent); pp. 8, 10 below, 24 right, and 26 (Press-Tige Pictures); pp. 10 above, 18, 22, 28 above, and 29 above (David Thompson); p. 15 below (Robert Burton); p. 24 left (Stephen Mills); p. 25 (Bruce A. Macdonald); p. 27 (Robin Redfern); Bruce Coleman Ltd. for p. 5 below (Jane Burton); p. 11 (Kim Taylor).

2 3 4 5 6 7 8 9 93 92 91 90 89